Breathe

By E.O.H. MacDonald

As a tribute to Florence, Mary, and Emily the women of my matriarchal lineage.

As a tribute to women everywhere...especially those who have endured injustice and pain.

Dedicated to Jesus Christ, the One who came to give men and women full, abundant lives.

Written by E.O.H. MacDonald

Designed and Illustrated by E.J. Duffield

Cover Photograph: iStockPhoto.com

Introduction

" People give pain, are callous and insensitive,
empty and cruel… but place heals the hurt, soothes
the outrage, fills the terrible vacuum that these
human beings make."

—Eudora Welty

This line of experiential journals, rich with motifs and images, is intended to create such places. I wrote them for myself because I needed them. Hesitantly sharing them with friends I discovered they needed them too. And so I offer them here, a collection of whimsical and everyday pieces, offered humbly from one friend to another, in the hopes they will help you create time and place to ask the kinds of questions you would like to ask…To become who you long to be and are designed to be.

Each entry is an opportunity to dig deeply into what it means to be creative, fun loving, deeply spiritual, deeply human, women… and to journey toward peace and wholeness.

Although each journal entry stands alone imagine them fitting together like a honeycomb cluster with open, interlocking angles. They represent ten years of my life. They are places that helped me explore the structure and symmetry of individual and community life. These were years of new experiences and learning to lay things down. As such they are bittersweet.

You can use the entries in any order. Pick and choose the ones that seem most relevant to you at this point in your life. Some are much shorter than others. Do not give them less time because of this.

These journals give you the opportunity to go deep. You may

wish to do this alone or with a trusted friend. Or you may find these exercises make a wonderful group experience, shared on a weekend away or over a series of Book Club-like discussion times.

Many of the sentences are deliberately long winded. They force us to slow down to read them. Try reading them once silently and again aloud to receive the full benefit.

Give yourself time to do the journal exercises— at least 1-2 hours for each. Add the questions I should have asked but didn't. Experiment with different mediums of expression— painting the colors of a reaction, making charcoal sketches of a sound, taking a tactile walk slowly touching everything you pass, using clay for sculpting, rock for building… Reconnecting with your senses and surroundings.

But most of all give yourself permission to…

Explore the wonder of self

Peek into the Divine

And Breathe.

Mosaic

S tepping carefully out of the slow moving boat I could feel layers
of fatigue, frustration and stress slipping away. I marveled at the
*ingenuity of marketing and service. First a horse drawn carriage down
a tree lined boulevard that literally forced you to lean back to gaze up
at the play of light filtering through the canopy; then a solitary punt
down a slow moving river past willow trees and grassy knolls. This was
already well worth the expense.*

*From the river rough cut stone steps, lined with ancient moss covered
urns filled with ferns and tiny white flowers, led to a wide verandah
covered with clinging vines. "Well done," I thought, "rolled Central
Park, the Thames River at Stratford and a Carolinian estate into one—
and somehow made it work."*

*The tiny, silver bells hanging inside the massive door gently
announced my arrival but there was no one else in the magical world I
had entered. The room reminded me of a quaint French café with lace
curtains and immaculately clean, crisp lines. Everything was polished
silver and white. Stainless steel and glass counters lined each side of the
hexagon shaped room. Above each counter were rows of shelves with
canisters and boxes of all shapes and sizes.*

In the center of the room, in sharp contrast to the rest, was a large aviary with luxurious foliage and brightly colored birds. They were tiny. Unlike any exotics I had ever seen. Not quite hummingbirds—although their iridescent plumage reminded me of hummingbirds. Not quite canaries or finches. I could not classify them. I closed my eyes for the umpteenth time in the last hour or so and listened to them sing. It was spectacular. Subtle and vibrant at the same time it forced me to hold my breath so as not to miss one note. I don't know how long I listened. Opening my eyes I tried to determine which sounds came from which birds. Watched their throats swell and pulse. They were oblivious to my presence, I, captivated by theirs.

Great translucent fan blades moved silently overhead. Above them the domed ceiling was lined with pressed tin like you might have seen in a turn of the century General Store. But this was no ordinary pressed tin. Starkly white it somehow gave the impression of a painting…each panel telling a different story. "They should put this stuff in doctor's offices," I thought, "it would make the waiting so much easier."

A woman was standing behind one of the counters. I had no idea how long she had been there. She looked up and beckoned me with a smile. In a white box in front of her were dozens of minute hard-candies. She pushed them back and forth with a paper-thin bamboo stick— making constantly changing, intricate patterns that were at once beautiful and enticing.

"Who are you?" she asked.

I began to introduce myself, thinking this was another step in the registration process.

She cut me short. "Not your name, who you are."

I didn't know what to answer. She waited— stick poised.

"I am a business woman…" I started, watching her face keenly for a reaction.

She did not move.

I tried again, "An entrepreneur." Nothing.

"I have two children," Silence.

My heart was pounding. What was she looking for?

"I am a woman." She smiled broadly and nodded.

"I am a weekend painter," I paused, "I love to cook."

"An artist," she murmured, beginning to rearrange the candies in front of her.

"Not an artist," I blurted out with an embarrassed laugh, "Just ... "

Her look stopped me immediately.

I looked inside myself and said with relief "I am an artist." It was strangely liberating.

"What else do you love?" she asked.

I looked around the room quickly for inspiration, "I love animals, and flowers of all kinds. Everything about them— the variety, the aroma…You know when I am walking past an arrangement I always sneak a secret 'whiff.'"

I was babbling. Yet she seemed completely at ease and listening intently.

"I love creeks in the woods and star lit nights— but everyone loves those of course."

"No they do not. Only people who love them love them." She said matter-of-factly.

I stared at her. This was so true. Why was I minimizing everything? I put aside the 'apologies and defenses' strategy.

I felt good— really good. This had been a good idea. She waited. I continued.

"I love good theater, collecting shells on the beach, early mornings in the country and late nights in the city, a good book and coffee in front of a fireplace on a rainy Saturday, the sound of pipe organs in old cathedrals, porch swings, hot showers and hot tubs…" I realized I was describing only experiences.

"I love new ideas and people willing to try them, grandparents who play with their grandchildren, friends who are loyal, people who really listen…I love freedom and beauty…health and energy."

"You are a woman who loves much and well."

In my heart I knew this was true.

I was not at all uncomfortable as I said, "I am a woman who loves freely. I hide my heart only because sometimes it hurts to have it."

"Yes," she said softly.

I felt completely calm and centered. She had no desire to know what I was not, what I could not do, who I could not emulate, where I had not been. Was she really the first person who had managed to communicate that to me in a way I could believe it? The thought astonished me.

"What type of woman are you?" she asked.

"I am the type of woman who works hard to make things better. I am the type of woman who gets angry easily, laughs easily and cries at little things. I am the type of woman who likes to have a few close friends and shares everything with them. I am the type of woman who votes every year— even when I think it futile."

She did not grimace. The candies were lining up in an exquisite pattern.

She pulled open a drawer with long sleeves of each shape and color carefully laid side by side. Selecting one tiny heart shaped one she slid it carefully out of the sleeve onto the counter in front of me.

"Raspberry," she said.

"My favorite," I whispered.

With the bamboo stick she lifted a pale yellow droplet from its sleeve and placed it in the palm of my hand.

"You are a strong woman— a brave and powerful woman. When you put this candy in your mouth think about the strengths you have that you have called weaknesses and tried so hard to hide. Later, when you find the creek to sit beside, place this raspberry one on your tongue and think about your heart and the many people and things it has nurtured."

She slid the drawer closed and pulled the lid over the box.

"What does the pattern mean?" I asked, afraid I had seen the last of it.

"This is the mosaic of what you have just told me. It will be ready for you when it is time for you to leave."

In that instant, I had an epiphany. I did not need enlightenment or self-discovery. I needed acceptance. She had not told me anything, she had merely thought the things I told her beautiful— so I could too.

I nodded, not knowing what to say, and opened the door she pointed to. It led into a magnificent garden. I was overwhelmed. I breathed deeply. Slowly the sounds of birds and insects began to differentiate themselves in my tumbled mind. After several moments I remembered the tiny treasures in the palm of my hand. Not far away was a bench under an oak tree. I had always loved oak trees, so strong and persevering. Born of a tiny acorn. Cute at best. Daring to have leaves unlike any other tree.

I settled in. The wood of the bench was graying from years of weather and use. The armrests reminded me of the granny rocker I had in my room. What stories could those arms tell of hands that had gripped them until they were polished and worn? How many other people had sat on this very bench? How many hearts needing healing, how many paradigms needing adjustment? It was good to sit here. Good to realize that I was alone but not the only one.

I placed the tiny yellow droplet on my tongue. Every sense jumped to a new level of awareness. Lemon. Perhaps lemon grass. Or was that a hint of mint? The flavor was subtle and poignant at the same time. Not sweet yet in no way tangy. It improved as it melted, changing ever so slightly every few seconds. How could anyone produce something so exquisite and package it in such a tiny bundle?

Strength, I was supposed to be thinking about strengths I had previously called weaknesses. "Supposed to be?" Where did that mindset come from? Years of school and business I supposed, or perhaps just years of life. I realigned my thinking. I was "able to be"… "privileged to be"… "relieved to be"… "excited to be" thinking about strengths I had called weaknesses. I sat quietly. What strengths did I see?

Images of myself at night kneeling to pray beside a sick child, opening doors— literally and figuratively— for other people, chatting with a lonely woman on a park bench, asking for forgiveness, laying aside an important project to listen, smiling at a nervous presenter to encourage them, crying in front of a great painting…image after image flashed through my head.

Had I seen these as weaknesses? Well they certainly did not show up on my resume.

But what about the deals I had closed, the impossible sales calls I had landed, the loans I had negotiated, the dissatisfied customers I had placated. These were strengths too. Ah, but I had known that they were strengths. These other images represented things I had dismissed. Ideas and moments when I had felt most unprepared, frightened and weak, or most like everyone else in the world. I could see it clearly. It was the mosaic of my life's strengths. The many sides of courage. The many sides of hope.

The candy was long gone but I did not move. I felt vulnerable, yet strong and deeply satisfied.

I don't know how long I sat there. I could not recount all the thoughts and images if I tried, for I have tried since.

I became aware that the sun had shifted and was now shining full in my face. I was warm. Too warm. I needed to move.

Half a dozen routes looked equally enticing. Which way to go? I chose the furthest path. Perhaps because I was experimenting today and it was somehow symbolic of how far I was willing to go to find myself. I was not disappointed in my choice. Perhaps they all led to the same places. I do not know, for I never had another chance to explore them. But this one led me past the very places I most needed to be. That much I know. My heart told me and I listened to it.

I found the brook the woman had promised. There were many beautiful spots to sit. I chose a mossy rock near a twist in the creek that forced the water to slow to round the inner corner and speed up at the outer edge. That's where I felt I was— at a twist in my journey. Some things were speeding up and some things were slowing down. I knew the stream was dropping sediment along the inner corner as it slowed and carving away at the outside corner as it picked up velocity. What was I dropping? What was I picking up?

I sat still for several moments— drinking in every detail. The sun through the trees. The stream bubbling over and around pebbles. I followed a leaf on its journey downstream— sometimes catching, sometimes spinning, and sometimes moving slowly on.

The raspberry candy! I had forgotten it. Somehow it had not melted in my hand. How long had I carried it for? I hesitated yet to put it into my mouth. I counted backwards from 100— why I don't really know. Then slowly placed it on my tongue. It was fresh and delicate. Subtle and rich. I remembered gathering raspberries as a child in the briars around the farm. The scratches were well worth the delight of finding the perfectly formed, deep red fruit. Hmm, another life lesson. OK, people and things my heart had nurtured.

My family certainly, friend's lives, projects I had dreamed into being, plants in my garden, people I had believed in, artists whose paintings I had admired, causes I had given to, ideas I had validated, project launches I had attended...lady bugs I had set on their feet, letters I had written to the editor, suggestions I had made to multiple bosses, jobs I had delegated when I wanted to hang on to them, creative ideas I had generated in brainstorming sessions...the list was longer then I would have thought. What an incredible idea to have within me the power to nurture or kill in so many different ways. I decided to nurture more and kill less.

It was turning cooler. Once again I had no idea how long I had sat there. I did not know what to do now. I remembered the mosaic I would take away with me. Would each candy be so rich? How would I know when to eat them? I hated the thought of destroying the pattern but dreaded even more the prospect of missing what insights those quiet moments might bring. Life is so much like that.

The woman was not there when I returned to the room. I guess I did not need her anymore. The box was waiting on the counter where she had left it. I knew it was mine. I recognized the pattern.

Inside the lid was a beautifully handwritten inscription.

"Do you think anything this intricate and exquisite formed by chance? Go find the Creator."

I carefully replaced the lid and carried the box out to the waiting punt. I knew the trip home would be as luxurious as the journey here— perhaps because I no longer feared the end of it.

The Beginning.

Journal Questions:

Find a quiet, beautiful place and journal using the following questions as starting points.

What part of this journey most appealed to you or did you most relate to? What was it that spoke to you?

Who are you? What words and images really describe who you truly are?

What do you love? Look deep within yourself to find the things that really matter to you— especially the ones you have dismissed as less important or more "common."

What type of person are you? What motivates you? What are you passionate about, faithful in, afraid of, and concerned about?

What strengths do you have that you have previously called weaknesses? What are the "other sides of your strengths"—the little things you have never celebrated?

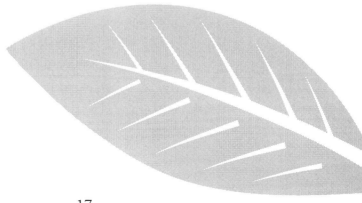

If your life is like a stream are you at a turn *(if so, what is speeding up and taking on new things and what is slowing down— what do you need to drop?)*, a straight stretch *(if so, what is flowing smoothly, where is it running too fast or too slow, what makes up the banks of your life to help keep you on track?)*, a watershed *(if so, what choices do you face that could take you in very divergent directions?)*, or a delta *(if so, what is your life or contribution flowing into or onto, what is it watering, what is it flooding)*?

What people and things have your heart nurtured? List them all.

Who affirms who you are? Cherishes you? Thinks that you are truly beautiful?

Who nurtures your soul?

Where have you looked for the Creator? In what ways might you be limiting yourself from finding a God that is not of your own making? i.e. bigger, deeper, more powerful, seeking more from you?

BREATHE

Suggested retreat places:

A statue garden

A good book of poetry

A National Park

A creek near you

A flower garden in any season

A monastery or retreat center nearby

A favorite art gallery or museum

A chair in front of a fireplace

A wicker rocker on a front porch

Add your own:

_____

_____

_____

_____

_____

_____

_____

_____

Time to Rebuild

I had never worked with mortar before— never held a trowel. But I wanted a garden wall and somehow I knew that I needed to be the one to build it. So I went to the quarry to choose the rock— running my hands across the rough cut stone, noticing the diversity of color and the reflection of light on the granite. Even the gravel looked beautiful up close. How could I have never noticed this before? At the local hardware store I got the tools and instructions I would need— how hard could it be? I could always plant ivy to cover any holes or bulges.

Little did I know how time consuming and back breaking this task would be. Little did I know how cathartic. With sweat dripping down my back and mosquitoes buzzing near my head and hands I had hour after hour of solitude, profound solitude, uninterrupted time to think. The rocks became symbols for me—each one intimately known as I found the right place for it, the right partners to support and frame it, the right side to present to the world and the right side to surrender to the ants and roots of the garden. They came to represent people or projects I was dealing with. Some were smooth and fit easily, stayed put.

Others proved more unwieldy, prone to wander, jagged and generally uncooperative. As the wall inched slowly upward, layer upon reworked layer, I processed slowly downward, layer upon reworked layer. Images from my adult, teenage and childhood years seeped randomly into my thinking.

Sometime mid-afternoon on the third day I hit rock bottom. There were holes in the foundation of my life that I did not know how to fill. No wonder everything built on top of it felt shaky and unprotected. No amount of mortar would hold this wall up. I knew it was time to rebuild. I returned to the hardware store and bought a sledgehammer. The biggest one I could find. I also bought new work gloves. The others had been building gloves. These were for demolition. I wrestled the sledgehammer into the trunk of my car and took the slow way home—needing time to contemplate what I was about to do. Half of my vacation was over and I was about to undo the fruit of it. Was this really necessary or just another overreaction? Stopping at the park to watch the children on the swing I knew I was not overreacting. I needed to face those stones one at a time. I needed to rebuild.

What had taken three days to build came down in as many minutes. I brought the top layer into my big country kitchen and set them on the windowsill. Might as well start with them. When rebuilding the wall around Jerusalem Nehemiah instructed the people to build the wall around their own home so as to ensure their vested interest in a job well done. I knew that this garden wall was really the wall around my own home, my inner self, my soul. I had a vested interest in it being secure as well as beautiful.

Week by week I alternated the rocks on my windowsill until each layer had sat there in the sun for my daily inspection. I had learned a lot about the hurdles and building stones of my life but I still needed a cornerstone, something to hang it all on, and something to hold it all together. I began to search the nearby fence lines and forests— not knowing what I was even looking for. I began to pray.

Then one rare lazy Saturday in my wanderings I found the ruins of an old fireplace, part of the chimney still jutting up out of the tall grasses that had overrun the site. I carefully traced the outline of the building moving the layers of debris that covered the old foundation. It had been a one-room building, no bigger than my living room. I sat facing the fireplace and tried to imagine the walls intact. My hands moved over the grass near the doorway, looking for clues. Then there it was, a dated cornerstone such as one sees on Heritage buildings. 1867. The year of Canada's Confederation. I was almost breathless. The year of conception. My cornerstone. My heritage.

Between the second and third number were three Greek letters that I traced with my fingers, feeling their importance. CMB. Where had I seen those before? My mind went back to a childhood memory of a starry night not long after Christmas and a candlelit service in grandma's country church. It was the celebration of Epiphany and on the way home we had traveled a new way—even as the wise men had——then written these letters in chalk over our front door. It had been a magical night, being out late, hearing the carols, pausing to write the letters over the door as snowflakes began to fall. But during the night a major blizzard had raged, wiping much of the chalk off the wall. Within weeks there was no trace left. What had those letters meant and why had we written them then? And if it was important enough to do at the time why had we never written them again?

I struggled to my feet with the stone in my arms then suddenly realized it did not belong to me–at least not yet. I drove to town going first to the library to research the three Greek letters. An ancient European tradition included writing these letters over the doorpost on the twelfth day of Christmas to celebrate the wise men's journey and the treasure they found under the star. CMB for Caspar, Melchior and Balthazar (the traditional names assigned to the Wise Men) and the Latin blessing "Christus Mansionsem Benedicat" - "May Christ bless this dwelling."

I asked the realtor to find the owner of the land that embraced the foundation for what I now believed had been a tiny country church. I asked her to make them an offer. Then I returned home to start rebuilding my wall… in anticipation of the cornerstone.

Journal Questions:

When was the last time you had a lazy Saturday to meander and how did you spend it?

What rocks from your garden wall need some time in the sun of your kitchen window for understanding and healing? What would that look like for you?

What events in your nation's history most resonate with you and why?

What memories trace the storyline of your heritage?

How would you diagram this?

What are you building? Why are you building it?

If you were to craft a lazy Saturday of meandering, what would it look like?

Tiny Treasures

Start some collections. Have you noticed how incredible and unique tiny seashells are? Start collecting shells or pebbles or beads or stickers or stamps or sugar packages from restaurants or buttons or anything tiny. If you need ideas try to look at the world through the eyes of a child. They know how to do this.

Journal Questions:

What did you collect as a child?

What does that suggest about you?

What did you collect as a teenager?

What does that tell you about yourself?

What did you collect as a young adult?

Why did you collect these?

What do you collect now?

What does this reveal?

If you could collect anything in the world what would it be? Why?

Sensations

*M*ango and lemon silk wafting in long tresses from bamboo poles…the scent of jasmine and marigold… a new sari laid carefully on the table.

Richly embroidered with gold and silver threads the delicate silk slid through my fingers as I tried again and again to gather and tuck it in place. Finally I pulled the tasseled bell pull and a tiny woman, with gently graying hair at her temples, wrapped the sari with deft and delicate movements.

Outside the pastel beams of the setting sun stroked the brilliant colors of the tents, blending them with the now emblazoned horizon. Men in white cottons lit thousands of tea lights along pathways and hung paper lanterns in the trees. Every pond and fountain sparkled with floating candles. Flower petals, strewn casually on the grass, captured the purples of the sun in their cupped hands while bees made their final tour of the garden before retiring.

It was magical.

The bracelets on my wrists and ankles felt cool and jingled as I walked. The rings on every finger and toe made me laugh. At home I rarely wore jewelry— here I was alive with it.

I wrapped the silk scarf tighter as the breeze chilled my shoulders and marveled at the warmth of the sand under my bare feet.

This was what my "urban tired," fast paced life was lacking— beauty that fed my senses and my soul. Breathing deeply I felt the constricting tightness of the sari against my ribs. I did not mind the tightness. At least this tightness was from without.

I chose a lime from the fruit table— shunning everything sweet and familiar in favor of that which would startle. The juice was refreshing and tart, poignant. Filling my scarf with papaya, star fruit and limes, and sprinkling them with flower petals, I made my way to the waterfall. Submerged lights reflected up through churning waters at the base and white moths circled above.

I sat on the straw mat feeling the rough texture of it through my light clothing. My breathing slowed yet I sat upright and alert. Taller than I ever had been before.

Some time later tea arrived on a bamboo platter with rice paper napkins and a fine china cup. I drank it very hot, delighting in the heat of it rushing through me.

How long had it been since I had truly felt? What processes— perpetual or infrequent— had driven this away? Or had it merely been left behind like so many other childlike things? I felt delight. Deep, powerful delight; and wonder. How long had it been since I had been in awe?

The music in the distance blended with that of the chimes hidden in the trees. I tried to separate the sounds and count the chimes but they seemed infinite. Was anything truly infinite? I sipped more tea and breathed in deeply. Where had I come from? Where was I going? I allowed these questions, lurking beneath the surface for months to come fully out now. They did not frighten me.

How could I hold onto mystery in the midst of the mundane? How could the rest of my life journey reflect the beauty of this retreat?

Later, I chose the boat closest to the dock because it was draped in white. The pole splashed through the shallow water and pushed against the muddy bottom. Eventually I got the hang of sliding it noiselessly into the water so as not to disturb the surface or startle the fish. This forced me to move ever more slowly—something I had not intentionally done in years. Each pole stroke was a conscious decision to do life differently—to find strength in fragile things, to peek into tiny wonders and to gaze boldly at life's mysteries. Eventually the boat stopped in the shallows of the opposite bank. I stepped out into the cool water and climbed up on the grassy knoll. Suspended between two willowy trees was a hammock. I reached into my bag and pulled out my plumed pen and journal...

Journal Questions:

What jewelry do I love to wear? How does it make me feel?

What flavor still startles and delights my taste buds?

How long has it been since I have truly felt? What processes— both perpetual and infrequent— are at work to numb my senses?

What *seems* infinite to me? What truly *is*?

Where have I come from? What are my roots— sociologically, physically, emotionally and spiritually?

Where am I going? Is what I am doing leading me towards who I want to become?

How can I hold onto mystery in the midst of the mundane?

What is my soul craving and where can I find refuge, refreshing and filling?

How will the rest of my life journey reflect the beauty my senses and soul find?

How would I paint the colors of this experience?

What symbols illustrate the wonder and delight I long to live?

What sounds need to be part of my day to remind me to slow down, fill up and flow out?

What will be different for me now?

And I Realized I Knew Nothing

One day I watch a middle-aged woman in a bookstore reassuring a severely disabled young man— her son. He is loud and obviously distraught. She is patient and calm. I think she has been here before. I wonder how many times. How many hours has she spent reassuring and teaching and explaining? Looking at my two healthy children I realize how little I know about parenting.

Another day I see a little person--— a woman who would stand perhaps 30 inches tall, if she could stand. Her crippled and shriveled legs barely balance her misshapen body and large head but her hair and makeup are perfect and she is out alone— in a motorized wheelchair— shopping at Christmas time. I imagine the stares, the comments, the questions, and the obstacles— the childhood—she has faced. And I wonder— what do I know about courage?

At a local fast food restaurant a woman with a very disfigured face and a purple lump where an eye should have been lumbers slowly from her table to the condiment stand— her head never raised to see the smile I long to give her. Could she have been like this from birth? Or is it the result of an accident or illness? Which would be harder to accept and to deal with? What do I know of loneliness?

The doctor of a woman with cancer and her daughter who seizures multiple times per day from unknown causes tells her that nothing can be done for either of them and that they must now go home and accept this fact. What do I know of disappointment?

A child is born addicted to cocaine because her mother was unable to overcome her habit for even a few months. She goes through withdrawal in the arms of a stranger. What do I know of pain?

Orphaned children, finally adopted by wealthy foreigners are turned back at the border— after months of negotiations and disappointments and hopes and prayers and waiting.

Terrorism and war claims parent after parent and son after son and lonely, heartbroken people finally stop yelling and cursing and crying because they have no will left.

Holocaust survivors... Prisoners of War... Severe Autism... Land mines and letter bombs... Child Prostitution... Human Trafficking... HIV/AIDS... Traumas and tragedies of inexplicable dimensions... I look at these things and realize that I know so very little.

" He has showed you, O man, what is good. And what does the Lord require of you? To act justly and to love mercy and to walk humbly with your God."

—Micah 6:8 (NIV)

Journal Questions:

What shows you how little you know about life?

Do you find that liberating or frustrating? Or both? And, if the latter, how have you learned to hold these opposites in each hand? Is there balance or tension?

How have you learned of courage?

How have you learned of peace?

How have you learned of waiting?

How have you learned of compassion?

How have you learned of love?

Found Moments

The telephone rang—waking me out of a rich deep sleep.

"How's the weather there?" asked a colleague when I picked it up.

I squinted to look out the window. It was beautiful. Sunny, cold and clear.

"There's a blizzard here. I'm calling off our meeting."

"Okay," I mumbled, not quite comprehending.

"What are you going to do with a free day?" she asked.

"I don't know."

My mind raced through all the projects and phone calls on my to-do list. I passed my briefcase in the hallway, carefully laid out last night in preparation for the early start I had anticipated for this morning. I poured a glass of orange juice and stood looking out the window. I took a deep breath.

"OK, what's most important?" I asked myself.

Always do the most important thing first. That's my mantra. I noticed a tiny chickadee huddled on a branch of the maple tree near the window. Its feathers were puffed up and its head pulled in trying to keep warm. I filled the birdfeeder, made a coffee and sat watching the birds discovering and cracking the sunflower seeds. I couldn't remember the last time I had filled it. I couldn't remember the last time I had taken the time to watch the birds. It felt luxurious. I remembered snow days at school, that wonderful feeling of unexpected freedom, a whole day to play.

I sat back and let the aroma of the coffee and the sound of the clock ticking lull me. This was the most important thing for me today. I needed a snow day. I made another cup and sprinkled cinnamon on top, something I usually only did when I went out for coffee. I gathered my housecoat around me and curled up in a chair, enjoying each sip, still watching the chickadees. I began to notice tiny differences in their behavior. Funny I had never thought about whether or not they had personalities or preferences, only their pecking order.

Suddenly the window was too great a barrier, like the difference between driving down a country road in an air conditioned car with the windows rolled up and riding a bicycle with a picnic in the wicker basket. In one you viewed the world. In the other you lived it. I pulled on sweats and boots and stepped quietly outside. The birds flew away but soon returned when I sat perfectly still.

"Wind chimes, I should get some of those," I thought. I've always loved the sound of wind chimes. I pulled out my camera and zoomed in on the birds. It took patience. They moved so quickly and unexpectedly, always fearful and alert, always working at survival, always getting out of the way of bigger, stronger birds. I wondered who might be watching me in the dance I called life. Who might be analyzing the moves and countermoves of my day? As the birds watched the ants and I watched the birds was Someone watching me? And if so what could They tell me from Their perspective? I longed for that wisdom…those insights…that big picture.

Waiting for the right lighting, angles and framing for my shots helped me sit long enough to deeply relax. The birds had become a way for me to step back and assess, to realign my priorities and to consider the cost of a life spent in frenzy. What was most important? If time was one of my most valuable commodities what was I spending my life on?

Back inside I journaled my thoughts. Not in a traditional lined notebook. I chose colorful unlined paper and wrote crosswise and in spirals and from corner to corner, forcing myself to process differently. I doodled all over the edges and pasted the pages inside my clothes cupboard where I would see them every morning while dressing. I did not want to soon forget the lessons of this snow day... this "found day." Who had found whom? I wondered.

Perhaps I would not have too many "found days" but I could build "found moments" into normal days. Amazing how excited this thought made me! I determined to spend a minute every day staring at something truly beautiful—a flower or sunset, a painting or child's face, poplar leaves moving in the breeze, the colors in a carpet—anything that was beautiful but that I might have merely glanced at before.

On an impulse I went to a music store and bought beautiful classical music and put it in my car in anticipation of the next traffic jam. I could hardly wait to have to listen to it. I slipped a tiny poetry book into my purse— not to be opened until the next lineup I had to wait in. A sketchpad and charcoal pencil to hide in my desk, scented liners for the dresser, candles and ferns for the bathroom, prints of the Masters greatest works for the den...I hid treasures in every conceivable spot...all ready for clandestine moments of oasis in the busyness of the day.

Was I forgetting anything? Friends. There were not enough "girl times" in my life. I pulled out my day-timer and scheduled in hot tub parties, hot chocolate and heart to hearts, a cooking class and a paper maché party. There was something very tactile about childhood crafts that appealed to my sense of fun. I wrote beautiful invitations to good friends and sprinkled in some people I wanted to get to know better.

Family. Was I wrapped up in doing when they needed me to be? Was I available to listen and to play? Did my aging father really need me to clean his house or should I focus my time with him on looking through photo albums and hearing stories? Had times of celebration become more about gifts than giving? Had hard times become more about coping than grieving? Had I lost touch with what it meant to be family in a world that struggled between independence and community?

Okay, what about work— a huge part of my life— what was most important there? What were the non-negotiables? The critical success factors? The things worth spending some of the best hours of my life on? This forced me to cut through so many seemingly important things for the few truly significant ones. I looked at my day-timer again and slashed several reactive activities. I built in buffer times, listening times, thinking times. I wrote PORTABLE DICTATING MACHINE on my birthday wish list. I wanted to be able to record the nuggets gleaned from conversations, middle of the night revelations and quiet reflective times more effectively.

I realized with a start that I had considered self first and not felt guilty about it. Was it because I knew that I soon would have no water left in the well to draw from? Was it because I was so desperately thirsty?

The steps I had taken were important but somehow I knew there was more. Was it possible that there was a deeper well I could tap into? A spring perhaps, that I had overlooked? I remembered watching the birds and wondering who was watching me. The birds became so accustomed to me they soon forgot I was there. Was it possible that in my fixation on my small world I had become oblivious to Someone watching over me? The birds had only to look around to see me— where did I need to look for that Spring of Living Water?

I started by asking out loud, "Spring of Living Water, help me to see You. I need to learn from You. I am thirsty."

A quiet assurance crept over me, the peace of knowing that all of life is a journey— that there are more-traveled and less-traveled paths to chose from that do in fact lead to different places— but that there was Someone who could see all the way to the end.

Journal Questions:

Chose an unlikely medium (charcoal, pencil crayons, a mural …) to express your thoughts on and reflect on these ideas.

In the movie *Sabrina* actress, Julia Ormond, asks Harrison Ford what he is doing with all the time he is "saving" by working instead of looking out the window of the plane. He replies that he is storing it up and she answers, "No you aren't."

What are you missing with the multitasking, timesaving, coping mechanisms you've built into life?

What treasures do you have hidden throughout your day? What could you schedule, let go of, or place that would allow you to enjoy "found moments" of your own?

If you are the primary home-maker in your home who creates a home for you?

How can you best capture your best thoughts and most beautiful insights? Where would you keep them? What would you do with them?

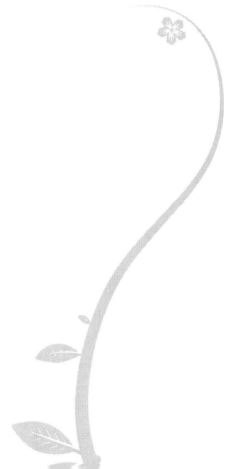

The Maze: On Finding Perspective

M *y rented Fiat crunched over the soft limestone chips as I rounded the corner and saw the castle through the trees that lined the drive. It was smaller than I had expected, infinitely smaller. I couldn't help feeling disappointed. Had I traveled half way around the world for this?*

No one met me at the door or helped carry my suitcase up the stone stairs to the top of the tower where my room was. There was a faint musty smell as I turned the old lock with one of the keys that had arrived with my confirmation. Strange that they sent the key on ahead...

18-foot high floor to ceiling windows on five of the six walls were draped with rich floral tapestries, held back by velvet tassels. A dozen pillows smothered the head of the gigantic bed. I threw them off immediately. They smothered me too. On the mantle of the dark wood fireplace was a stuffed peacock. I couldn't bear it and hid it in the only closet I could find.

The en suite bath had luxurious towel warmers and a tub on giant bronze lion paws. Tiny windows cranked open to reveal clay-roofing tiles on a Mary Poppin's style roof with slopes and railings and walkways. Did I dare climb out?

Grasping the narrow windowsill I put one foot on the tub and stretched the other up towards the sink just as a very official knock sounded on my door. I hesitated... the knock came again. Stepping down I opened the door to find a huge basket of fruit, dinner menu and bouquet of greenery on a white damask cloth covered trolley. I wheeled it inside my room, checking over my shoulder to see who might have brought it, no one there.

The greenery was magnificent— every manner of bough and branch— the aroma of Christmas and forests after a rain and blue spruce...Prickly hemlock and holly interspersed with boxwood and soft white pine. This is what belonged on the fireplace. I carefully positioned it, allowing the pine boughs to overflow the mantle. Not a single flower or ornament yet I had never seen anything so beautiful.

Looking out the window I realized there were in fact no flower gardens at all as far as I could see. Just trees and bushes of every description. And, of course, somewhere on this vast lawn, the maze, decades old and tirelessly maintained. Perhaps after dinner I would check it out. What would one wear to dinner in this castle retreat? I checked the menu for clues. "Dinner will be served to your room at 8 pm." My room? Strange again— I had not ordered room service. I picked up the phone— no service. Oh well, it would be more relaxing that way.

There were no clocks in the room and as usual I had forgotten to bring one. Thinking I must have a least an hour until dinner I plopped down on the overstuffed couch and picked up a hard cover book with richly textured, hand made paper. Every page was blank except for the inscription "Sketches." Another book read "Thoughts" and a final one "Prayers." Nice touch. I chose a piece of charcoal and began to scribble *a rough sketch of the room as a reminder since no cameras of any kind were permitted. It was poorly done. I put the book down.*

The bathroom window! I had forgotten. Hovering with one foot still on the sink I squeezed out the tiny window onto the tiled roof. The view was incredible. I sat down, not daring to go further until I became accustomed to the height. The tower beside me stretched up another 20 feet. I was sitting on the roof of the castle proper. There were catwalks in three directions. I took the one furthest from the edge, promising myself that they must be safe. The railings were not tall enough to reach when standing so I walked bent over, eyeing the rusty fittings and fragile looking struts. Soon I could see the lawn that could not be viewed from my room— another vast expanse of green— and quite a distance from the castle was a long hedge that must be the outer wall of the maze. I sat down again.

Perhaps it had been a good idea to come here after all. Not a single person on the green. The sun was just starting to set beyond the hills and the colors in the sky were rich and merciless. Did sunsets always look like this? "Tomorrow night I'll bring those pastels," I promised myself. I tried to get my bearings. "This must be west. So my room faces east. I will see the sunrise in the morning."

It began to cool and as I stood to retrace my steps I realized I must have sat unmoving for a long time. The stiffness in my joints and the darkness in the air suggested an hour or more. Beyond the crest of the roof it was much more difficult to see and I felt my way along, terrified of a misplaced step. It was much harder to get back in the window than it had been to get out. I wonder how long it would take someone to find me out here? Finally I managed, somewhat scraped and bruised, to climb back in.

It had been worth it. Definitely.

Dinner was already in front of the fireplace. How long it had been there I had no idea but even with its elaborate covers it was no longer warm. No matter, it tasted delicious, perhaps anything would have. I closed my eyes. Subtle flavors of orange and maple syrup in the sauce. Slivers of root vegetables…blue potatoes. Cheesecake to die for…with plump raspberries and blackberries piled on top. Black, strong coffee, somehow still hot. I drank it… not worrying that it might keep me up. What difference did it make when I slept or woke?

I ventured out into the dark hall, wanting to stretch before bed. There were candles lit every 10 feet or so, giving the halls neither a romantic nor an eerie look. It was rather the norm. I explored the floors below me— now half hoping to meet someone— but returned to my room 20 minutes later having not seen a soul. "I'll meet some people tomorrow," I thought, sinking into bed.

The flames in the fireplace had burned down to embers and I watched them for several peaceful moments before falling off to sleep. Tomorrow I would tackle the maze for the first time.

Thankfully I had not thought to shut the curtains so light flooded into my room in the morning and I awoke more refreshed than I had been in years. Could one good sleep do that? What might two weeks do?

A white envelope slid under my door. I waited a minute and then got up to see what it was. The breakfast menu and another key… I opened the door. Freshly squeezed orange juice, papaya and mango salad with a light mint sauce, crisp toast triangles and more delicious, jet-black coffee. I ate in my pajamas, savoring the luxury. Might all the meals be delivered like this? I'd have to check into it— if I could ever find anyone to ask.

What could the other key be for? A work out room perhaps? Or an outside door? I'd take it with me when I went out. I pulled out new thick socks and the hand knit sweater my grandmother had sent just before I left, determined to be as comfortable as possible.

Then I climbed down the many stairs and searched the whole first floor for a front desk or concierge or something. Nothing. No one.

Giving up I started for the maze. It was further than it looked and I stopped twice to rest along the way. I didn't know I was in this bad shape! Starting today that all changes.

I wanted to walk around the outside of the maze to get a sense of its size but found that impossible as it bordered a marshy area that could not be easily negotiated. There was more than one entrance. This surprised me. I peeked in each one before deciding to start with the closest. It was truly delightful. Eight-foot high lush green walls on either side and soft short grass under foot. I set out determined to master it the first day. There must be a pattern. A trick. I'd find it.

I started by memorizing corners, keeping track of the sun overhead in an attempt to judge direction. Every few minutes I retraced my steps to ensure I could get out. I'm not claustrophobic just cautious.

The sun was high in the sky now and it was difficult to tell directions by it anymore. I decided to quit for the day. I hated to admit defeat but I was getting nowhere. I had tried each entrance and every strategy I could think of. At least three hours had passed. I was hot and tired.

Half way back to the castle I began to wonder if I had missed lunch. My stomach was growling. Just ahead I saw a picnic spread under a willow. What a great idea. I'd have to arrange for that for tomorrow. As I got closer— wondering if I could sneak a strawberry without anyone noticing (there was no one in sight anyway)— I realized the reserved sign had my name on it. How wonderful! They thought of everything!

I did not conquer the maze on that first day; or on the next or the next. It frustrated me beyond belief and became a metaphor for the issues in my life that had sent me on this retreat in the first place. I had to conquer it. Somehow I knew my spirit needed that confirmation. And yet day after day it beat me. I had taken to drawing maps and charting potential courses as I became more and more familiar with the three entrances and the multiple turns inside. Late at night I sat on the roof and schemed. But time was almost up.

I had not yet seen another person on the grounds or in the castle yet my room was always refreshed when I returned and every meal was delivered just when and where I needed it. I felt no desire to leave the grounds. The waterfalls, walk ways and maze were sufficient stimulus for me. Having explored them for more then a week I felt I had not yet begun to see them. Everything that I needed— everything I wanted right now— was here. The journal and sketchpads were almost filled with my scribbles, each depicting a moment or thought that now seemed like pearls on a string to me. Strange as it seems now I was neither lonely nor bored.

Early one morning, after strawberries and fresh cream I took my coffee and journal and headed for the maze. I had determined that this would be my last attempt. Frankly I had lost the zeal for victory. Frustration now outweighed my need to succeed. I sat under a huge tree with spreading branches, finishing my coffee and half-heartedly plotting a strategy. As I did so I looked up into the deep canopy above me. A flash of insight. Quite obviously I was trying to tweak an inherently flawed approach— just like my life, I thought. I needed a fresh perspective. I began to climb. I have never been a tree climber even as a child I was clumsy at best. I knew it was foolish. What if I fell? I climbed on. Clutching for hand holds in the deeply textured bark I often cut my fingers and scratched my arms and legs. No matter. I climbed on. I found myself going around and around the tree in my quest for the best route.

Far beneath me my shoes were carefully placed in the hopes I would be able to put them on again if I ever got down. I stopped frequently, breathed deeply, began to smell the tree and appreciate its incredible complexity. It was truly a magnificent tree. I was delighted to be climbing it. Each leaf was so similar and yet different. I had reached the highest point I could trust my weight to so I carefully nestled into a nook and strained around to see the maze. Contrary to expectation I could not see it clearly, the angle and leaves obstructed the view. If I waited for the wind to blow the upper branches I could see different bits and piece them together.

It was an amazing sight. Easily two hundred feet across and a beautiful network of passageways and dead ends. Try as I might I could not chart a course that took me through it. I kept ending up back where I had started. In fact each of the three entrances seemed plagued with the same problem— they lead in circles. Was it designed to frustrate already frustrated pilgrims like myself? I was now very uncomfortable and turned to climb down when I noticed that someone had been in this spot before me. Carved in the branch near the spot my hand had rested were the words:

"THE FASTER WE RUN IN CIRCLES

THE SOONER WE COME BACK

TO THAT WHICH WE SOUGHT TO FLEE."

Now that was worth a fresh page in my journal— or perhaps a whole new journal! I scrambled down the tree…

Journal questions:

What parts of this story most attracted me? What did it make me crave? What did it make me wonder?

What feels like a maze to me?

Is it only in times of deep aloneness that I can see my own soul? Hear my own voice? Read my own thoughts? Why then do I spend so much time avoiding solitude? Is it the fear of what is there or the fear of what isn't?

What am I most afraid I might find in the deep places of my heart?

What am I most afraid might be missing?

What am I running from?

What am I running to?

What circles do I keep running in and where are they taking me?

Where do I need perspective? What "trees" are there in my life that might provide it?

What words of wisdom would be scribbled there that would give me fresh insight?

What words of wisdom would I leave for the next climber?

Describe a perfect time of solitude— what setting, scenery, foods, and activities would it have? What would definitely not be there?

What would I learn if I spent two uninterrupted weeks in that place?

A Silky Blue Ribbon

I remember the day I bought that length of silky blue ribbon. It was a bit out of my price range but it was just so pretty. I could imagine it tied in a bow around a basket of dried flowers or hanging behind a trilogy of pictures on the gray-blue walls of the living room.

When I had gotten home that day I'd carefully tucked the tissue paper wrapped ribbon into a drawer to be drawn out and admired until I had found the perfect home for it.

Several days later, while I was out working in the garden, my young son was growing frustrated trying to fly his new kite.

"Perhaps it needs a longer tail," I suggested casually, so as not to seem critical.

"I like this tail," he retorted abruptly.

I said nothing else. After several more attempts he apparently gave up and withdrew into the house in disgust.

Engrossed in my weeding I did not notice him reappear a few minutes later. In fact it was not until he called out, "It's flying!"

with great excitement, that I looked up. The sky had never looked so blue. The silver kite was beautiful soaring against such a backdrop. And the tail...it was magnificent...streaming out behind the kite like two long silky ribbons.

"Ribbons?" I whispered. I paused. I had never dreamed they would look so perfect. How much better against the sky than on a wall or basket! How like a child to create real art. I was glad I had bought such expensive ribbon. This masterpiece deserved it.

"I like the tail," I said.

He smiled, "So do I."

Journal Questions:

What "special things" are you saving for a rainy day that might never come? What might it mean for you if you created masterpieces from them now?

Describe a time when someone used their special teacups or china plates or well aged wine or anything they had "saved for a special day" for an otherwise ordinary time with you. How did that make you feel?

A beautiful piece of ribbon or paper or glass can re-energize and re-inspire... a word of encouragement, a poem that has been percolating in the back of your mind or a knitted afghan meant for someone who needs warmth even more so...

Who, in your circle, needs a silky blue ribbon today?

Snapshots

One year I collected memories without tangible reminders. That meant I had to memorize the scene and lock it away for instant recall when needed. I chose to remember a few places—like an island surrounded by mist one early morning on a lake in Muskoka, Ontario, Canada. It was so ethereal. I sat for a long time soaking it in and can recall almost every detail even now if I close my eyes.

That was the year we were to go on a three month sabbatical. We set out in an old converted school bus, which, because we worked on it literally up to the moment we left, had never been road tested. Rattling down the first bumpy road we discovered the cupboards wouldn't stay closed and schoolbooks, winter coats, the toaster and all the other accoutrements of a 3-month long family trip kept spilling out. Before returning home we would take a saw to the table, install "bungy cords" to keep the kids from falling out of bed, duct tape a Christmas tree to the counter and regret our decision not to take the time to add a source of running water.

But before that, on day two of our adventure in fact, my mother died suddenly and we returned home to be with my father. Who could have known how painful that would be. For my mother I wrote these journals. For my father, years later, I would write our family story. This was my way to thank them and to process their loss. May way to honor their memory.

When we finally set out some weeks later all our plans and priorities had changed. We set out on a new road, with no set destination or agenda.

For someone who has learned to cope with life by organizing, strategizing and perfecting this can be difficult. That journey would teach me more than I realized.

Friends wondered how we survived 3 months of "togetherness" in such an enclosed space and were amazed when I answered that, in a flash, I would turn around and do it again. Who in their right mind exchanges twenty-two-thousand square feet of a beautiful home for a 6'x12' traveling road show? Someone who has learned to love the freedom and simplicity it affords.

Looking back now I realize we marked time by the carefully chosen coffee stops and "skyscapes"along the way. There was the beautiful rustic square timber coffee house beside the icy cold mountain stream nestled in the mountains of California and the sidewalk café at La Jolla Beach where we sat in the sun and listened to live jazz music. There was the coffee shop on the main street of Ventura that had a huge indoor water fountain and massive murals of frogs on the walls, where the smell of cinnamon and chocolate rose from the coffee to fill our noses with delight.

And the sky— I can still see the clear crisp night we sat in a hot tub in El Paso, Texas and watched the stars under gently swaying palm trees. Or the time we drove across the plains of Montana and experienced a "Big Sky" for the first time. The contrast of the sharp blue expanse and the brilliantly white clouds left me with the same sense of awe as the first time seeing a true masterpiece of any kind. There were storms of incredible fierceness. There was the incredible stillness of the middle of the day in the desert.

There was the sensation of tobogganing down sand dunes in Arizona, the wonder of watching otters play off the coast of California, the simple pleasure of collecting shells on the beaches of Florida's islands... all these years later I can see and smell and taste these snapshot memories.

Journal Questions:

How do you mark time—by the number of days until pay day, the number of hours until quitting, the number of assignments left to accomplish…?

What were the highlights of your last vacation?

Last "work week"?

Last family time?

Last time alone?

How could you capture these images so as never to forget them?

How would you like to mark time for the next three months? By the number of sunsets you can see this year, the late night conversations you can share with people you care about, the gifts you give to people who least expect them...?

Close your eyes. What snapshots can you bring to mind of good memories?

What do they tell you about your life?

About yourself?

About your future?

Xania

*I*t had taken twenty-eight hours of travel to get here but, as I sat under the vanilla colored umbrella beside the fresh water fountain that made the town famous, it was well worth it. It was in fact surreal. Orthodox clerics, wild dogs, children and young lovers strode past the bouzouki player. I had stopped with others in the crowd when he first started to play and joined the brave ones who raised their hands or linked arms and danced in half circles around this mesmerizing sound.

But now I sit alone at my table. To my right five gentlemen, apparently inhabiting their regular table, philosophize and laugh loudly. The smoke from their cigars mixes with the richness of other aromas of sea and fishing boats and garlic and humanity and becomes delicious.

The stark angles of the white dolomite buildings contrast with the blue-black sky and the yellow with green trim studio apartment across the street— all lights on, all windows wide open.

Closing my eyes to lock that memory away I hear the sound of the waves against the breakwater and remember the blue of the Mediterranean over which I flew earlier. Artists from all over the world come to Crete to study the color blue— even as they visit Italy to study light. I had come to study other things, things deep within myself.

I was dining at 10 pm, like the locals. Taziki with lush tomatoes, olives and cucumber, then salad with sesame seeds, roasted red pepper and more cucumber, fish with lightly seasoned vegetables—everything swimming in succulent olive oil— topped off with one of the oversized ice cream dishes that looked more like a child's toy than a dessert. A tiny cup of strong Greek coffee followed by a sip of raki that burned in an absolutely delightful way counterbalancing the sweet candied apricot accompanying it. Full was not nearly a sufficient word to describe how I felt.

It felt good to be sitting still after three flights and the harrowing drive through narrow streets filled with cars, pedestrians, and motorcycles. The directions had seemed simple in the email, until you realized that many streets had no signs or, worse yet several. Besides, the ones in my directions had been blocked off to create pedestrian malls.

After stopping several times and finding people with varying levels of English (admittedly all better than my Greek) I had found the right street— confirmed by a jeweler who spoke perfect English and said,

"Yes this is the street you want"

"But it is blocked off"

"Yes it is forbidden."

"Then how will I get to my hotel?"

"You will have to go another way."

I finally parked near the sea under a huge tree and walked through a labyrinth of alleyways past tiny shops and sidewalk café's until I reached the street where I had talked to the jeweler. At the end of the street were *a dozen restaurants with outdoor tables covered in white table clothes and maitre d's expounding their virtues to potential customers, shooing away gypsies and constantly rearranging the furniture to make it look more inviting. Everywhere fathers— portly, stern and dependable; strong and opinionated; lovers of beauty and fine wine— watched the crowds and shooed away their wives and children.*

One maitre'd had sent me back the way I'd come, stopping for clarification another sent me back again, and back and forth until finally, just when I was truly exasperated, someone recognized the address and pointed out a tiny cobblestone alleyway just past the fountain.

On the ground floor of the narrow three-story building the owner painted vibrant reproductions of Byzantine icons. Golds, reds and rusts monopolized her palette. A narrow staircase wound up to the 7 rooms and roof top garden from which you could look down on the grape covered arbors below.

I had told them I was coming to celebrate an anniversary so the bed was strewn with bougainvillea flowers and there was champagne in a silver urn. Why had I not corrected them? Wasn't the whole purpose of this trip to come to grips with being alone?

Exhausted, I fell fast asleep only to awaken 3 hours later. The sheets and duvet were luxurious. I read for several hours then slept again. When I awoke the sun was pouring in through the solid wooden shutters I had left propped open. Looking down I watched a cat lazily washing itself in the sun, which was high overhead— I had slept until noon.

More alert than last night I now looked carefully at my room. Polished hardwood floors, a cream-colored antique settee, gauzy fabric hanging from each corner of the damask covered four-poster bed, twelve-foot ceilings. It was truly beautiful.

From the rooftop garden I watched the sailboats on the sea and listened to the friendly skirmishes between shopkeepers in the narrow lanes on either side.

Four doors down, an old ruined building had been turned into an outdoor restaurant. Tables were set amongst fallen pillars and atop the partially destroyed and now roofless second story. Ingenious. At night, lit only be candles, it would be magical.

All afternoon I explored the winding alleys…popping in and out of shops. Beautiful silver jewelry. Quaint brass coffee grinders. Gorgeous shawls and scarves…

After a second glorious sleep in I mounted an expedition into the mountains. Winding roads, once goat paths, and now racetracks for motorcycles took me past wild rosemary bushes, centuries old olive groves and fig trees. An ancient mosaic guarded only by a wooden rail fence to keep the animals off. An ancient pillar, now built into the end of someone's garden wall. An ancient church, still beckoning the faithful with its rich deep bell tones, an outdoor café built beside a trickling waterfall…all in just one small village.

But at some point I must stop exploring this unbelievable outdoor world and take a look at my inside one. Did I dare?

Traveling alone in a new country was not nearly as lonely as traveling alone into my heart. There were no friendly maitre d's or jewelry shop owners standing in their doorway. Or were there?

The next morning I began to retrace my steps. But this time I took a journal with me. Every kind person I met was asked the same questions—how had they dealt with the losses of their life? How did they find joy and purpose? Every beautiful spot became a place of quiet meditation. What did the places I chose have to say to me? About me? About my loss?

What did these fabulous people, quick to express emotion, have to teach me, an introverted Canadian?

Why could I cry more easily here with strangers than at home with those who loved me most?

Nearby Malta was the island where Paul of the Bible was shipwrecked.

Crete, the island where Zorba the Greek— the tale of an explosive man, larger than life— was written.

One of the few historically documented matriarchies was in Crete.

The first labyrinth was here— deep in the Knosses.

All along the roadside are little chapels and places for reflection. What is it about this combination of events and environments that made me know this was where I needed to come to heal?

Journal Questions:

If there were one place in the world you would want to go for healing where would it be?

What is it about Europe that attracts you?

About the Orient?

About the Mediterranean?

About the North?

About South America?

About the West Indies?

What elements about the place would be important?

Why do you think each continent has developed so uniquely? What does this teach us about humanity? Divinity?

How do you make important choices?

What does that teach you about yourself?

If someone asked you how you carry on after experiencing a deep loss what would you say?

Of Clouds and Calculations

It was a beautiful spring day. The kind that draws you outside after a long winter and won't let you go back in. It was calling me. But I was ignoring it. In fact, I was being disciplined, responsible, and persistent. I was listening to several tedious tapes in the hopes of finishing my most recent university correspondence course before the deadline.

My children, not understanding such foolishness yet, kept calling me to come out. Kept asking me to play.

"I'll play with you later, as soon as I get these tapes finished." I explained over and over.

As they ran outside laughing and pushing I secretly wished I could go with them. This course held so little relevance for me. It was a required credit I had left 'til the end in the hopes it would go away. What is worse, the professor droning into the tape recorder and assigning the lengthy assignments seemed to know, and not care, that this was the motive behind our enrollment. He made no discernable effort to make the course interesting or truly educational. It was tedious, difficult and seemingly incomprehensible. But I had to listen to the tapes, bluff my way through the assignment and memorize what seemed like important points for the exam. That's how it works.

After a seeming eternity I finished, rubbed my aching shoulders, stretched my cramped legs and flexed my stiff fingers.

"Take that!" I said with satisfaction, turning off the tape recorder with a flourish.

What a relief to join the children on the front lawn. We sat under a shady tree and watched the clouds. This inspired us to get some watercolors and attempt to paint them. Sitting at the picnic table we were amazed that something so simple looking in nature could be so difficult to recreate on paper. We wondered at how many possible combinations of color there could be in a sky, or how many shapes of clouds.

When the wind picked up and the paper blew we ran to get our new kites. We laughed and squealed when the wind caught them and fought with us for control.

"How strong the wind is!" we agreed. How inspiring to feel its strength for ourselves.

After a while, we tired of that game. Long before the wind did. So we took our kites inside and brought out little plastic boats to sail in the stream still swelling from the runoff. Tossing and turning their way down its course we noticed the way eddies trapped them and marveled at the tremendous force of moving water. We caught water striders and mossy sticks, and played with the 'skin' that 'grows' on the top of water—supporting objects both animate and inanimate.

Finally, exhausted, we lay back on the cool grass under the tree again and practiced our spelling words and multiplication tables.

"What course were you working on Mommy?" my son suddenly

asked.

"Just one of the courses I have to take for my Environmental Studies Degree pet," I answered.

"Oh," he said, nodding his head wisely, "I see."

Did he? Could he see the irony of it, as I could all of a sudden? Or was he still too un-indoctrinated? How thankful I was for such great teachers. Through their eyes I knew I still had a lot of "important stuff" to learn.

Journal Questions:

What lessons have children taught you?

What lessons did you learn as a child that still guide you?

What lessons from childhood are you ignoring?

If you could chat with the 5-year-old you what would she tell you?

What things about you would impress her?

What would seem curious to her?

What would she laugh at?

What would you tell her?

Sculpting Our Fears

*F*aced *with the biggest challenge of my life it was time to face some fears...*

The sculpture garden was a delight to my starved senses. The smell of the juniper and lavender. The rough bark of the century old oaks. The swaying grasses and curving pathways. Where to look first?

Unable to decide I sunk onto the rich, well kept lawn and lay back, soaking in the sun and listening to the song birds. My heartbeat slowed and I became aware of the breeze barely moving the tiny hairs on my arms.

Tall, ivy covered brick walls both framed and protected this oasis. Set off. Set apart. In the distance swans and ducks floated on a lily-studded pond. A lonely heron standing guard.

I was ready now and meandered through the gardens, stopping in front of each sculpture to name it for myself. This one was Darkness. This one Power. This one Failure, and the one nearby Illness. I found a place where all four sculptures I had chosen were visible. Bringing out the clay I pounded and stretched it—driving my thumbs deeply into it and leaving scratch marks where my fingernails dug mercilessly in.

The clay felt cool and responsive. It could be pummeled or patted into shape. I alternated between the two techniques, finally settling down to recreate each statue as closely as I could, examining the model and my version of it from every possible angle until I was satisfied.

I had come to reshape my fears but first I had to identify them. These were my enemies and I allowed myself to hate them. It felt good to stop pretending. Exaggerating the angular edges and sharpening the angles...experimenting with the sensation of color by creating crevices for shadows and smooth round surfaces for highlights. Hours passed.

How can darkness be reframed? Is darkness really on the same continuum as light or is it something completely different? How does darkness become light? Can it do so on its own? Better yet— what in darkness is beautiful and creative and comforting? An infant in a womb lives in darkness. A caterpillar waits in darkness in its cocoon. What is it that hides in darkness that frightens me? What is it that darkness reveals? If I were to remold this sculpture into a darkness that I could live with what would it need to be?

In a far off corner an old gardener knelt in the dirt. He seemed oblivious to me. Spotting him for the first time I turned my back towards his corner and focused on the clay.

I have seen so many abuses of power. Was there truly a positive side to it? Or was that another illusion that I, like so many others, held on to? Which was more fearful— failing or succeeding— and the responsibility that came with each? Why did I turn from success when it was finally within reach? Why did I set such illusive goals? How would I mold this? How was it molding me? Who pummels the clay of my life? Whose lives have I put my thumbprints into?

I fear hatred. Pure, malicious, wounded hatred. But wasn't love frightening too? The truer it was the more consuming and costly. I had never thought of love as something to be feared but here it was in front of me now. What is the face of hatred? The face of love? How could one possibly begin to mold them? Let alone transform them?

It is not just the overwhelming tasks but the relationships, the responsibility of leading real people with lives and responsibilities of their own that frightens me. The longer I lead the more I know this to be true. The more it shapes my thinking and decisions.

My legs and back began to ache. My fingers were stiff and cold. I moved to a tiered fountain that had seemed inviting before. Studying it more carefully now I see the gargoyles around the top spitting water down to the second level and the three fish shaped pieces that sifted the turbulent water and channeled it into a calm spillover pool where a constant sheet of water filled an irrigation system that ran along shallow aqueducts to the furthest corners of the garden. The sides of the aqueducts were green with slimy organisms. I pondered it for a long time then slowly approached the gardener who was still working in the same bed of greenery.

"How long have you worked here?"

"Oh, forever," he answered smiling slightly.

"Who made the fountain in the middle there?"

"I did."

"You're a sculptor?"

"Yes."

"Then why...?" I stopped myself. "And a gardener?"

"Same work, different medium."

"What is the fountain meant to represent?"

"The source of life giving water."

"But the source is hidden."

"Yes."

"And the outlets are kind of scary looking."

"Yes."

Gathering courage I said, "I am trying to refashion some models."

"Yes I know."

"I can't quite get them."

"It takes practice."

"Yes."

Pause.

"Perhaps you don't feel them enough yet."

" Perhaps. Or maybe I feel them too much," I said.

"Hmmm. Could be. Either way it takes more time than you have given it."

"More time?"

"Lots more time."

"I don't have much time."

"You have other things that are more important?"

I looked at him closely. He was not mocking me or judging, just asking.

"Actually I guess not."

"Why don't you stay in that cottage for a few days. That way you can look at them in every light."

I followed his eyes to a ramshackle, moss-covered shack hidden behind tall blackberry bushes. Bees buzzed contentedly from bush to bush. An overflowing window box hung beside the heavy wooden door. Turning to ask another question I saw that the gardener had gone—pushing his wheelbarrow slowly in front of him.

Why not peek in at least? A little round table held lumps of clay and sculpting tools. I was obviously not the first person to come here for creative refuge. In fact, the walls were lined with signatures. I moved closer to read some. "Going to tell her I love her John H., June 4th 1967... Back to school at 43—why not? Karen, Sept. 1981... Time to move on, Sam... If I make it I will be back to sign my name..."

Hundreds of life stories, now encapsulated in a few words, covering the walls and spilling over onto the back of the door and roof rafters. I reverently touched the chair and table. Hundreds of people had made decisions right here—faced their fears right here—gone out into the world from right here. It felt good to be alone yet not. I knew I had some work to do—deep soul work of which the clay was only one vessel.

But at least I had begun...

Journal Questions:

"I had come to reshape my fears but first I had to identify them. These were my enemies and I allowed myself to hate them. It felt good to stop pretending. Exaggerating the angular edges and sharpening the angles... experimenting with the sensation of color by creating crevices for shadows and smooth round surfaces for highlights."

Can I identify my fears? How would I name them?

If I were going to sculpt them what would they look like?

"How can darkness be reframed? Is darkness really on the same continuum as light or is it something completely different? How does darkness become light? Can it do so on its own? Better yet— what in darkness is beautiful and creative and comforting? An infant in a womb lives in darkness. A caterpillar waits in darkness in its cocoon."

What is it that hides in darkness that frightens me?

What is it that darkness reveals?

If I were to remold this sculpture into a darkness that I could live with what would it need to be?

"I have seen so many abuses of power. Was there truly a positive side to it? Or was that another illusion that I, like so many others, held on to?"

How has power— in my life or others— shaped me?

Where do I, without intending to maybe, abuse my power? Am I more apt to do this aggressively, passively, secretly, overtly, with "good intentions", when I feel I am "losing control"…?

Which is more fearful— failing or succeeding— and the responsibility that come with each?

Do I ever I turn from success when it was finally within reach? Why?

Am I more apt to set achievable or illusive goals? Or do I shun goal setting altogether? If so is this a healthy "I'm more of a problem solver" type of thing or an unhealthy "if I set goals I might have to work for them or worse yet, might work for them and fail?"

How are my goals, or lack thereof, it molding me?

Who pummels the clay of my life?

Read *Isaiah 64:8* from your favorite translation of the Bible

Whose lives have I put my thumbprints into?

"I fear hatred. Pure, malicious, wounded hatred. But wasn't love frightening too? The truer it was the more consuming and costly. I had never thought of love as something to be feared but here it was in front of me now. What is the face of hatred? The face of love? How could one possibly begin to mold them—let alone transform them?"

What is it about love I fear?

How would I describe the face of love?

Read *John 3:16*

How would I describe the face of hatred?

Where do I know pure love?

Read *1 John 3:1, 16, 18, 23*

Where have I felt hatred?

How are these two forces molding me now?

"It is not just the overwhelming tasks but the relationships, the responsibility of leading real people with lives and responsibilities of their own that frightens me. The longer I lead the more I know this to be true. The more it shapes my thinking and decisions."

What is it about leading others that is fearful? Joyful? Depleting? Life giving?

How am I using the influence I have to impact my world?

"The source of life giving water."

"But the source is hidden."

"Yes."

"And the outlets are kind of scary looking."

"Yes."

Gathering her courage she said, "I am trying to refashion some models."

"Yes I know."

"I can't quite get them."

"It takes practice."

"Yes."

Pause.

"Perhaps you don't feel them enough yet."

" Perhaps. Or maybe I feel them too much," I said.

"Hmmm. Could be. Either way it takes more time than you have given it."

How is the source of living water hidden? Where do I catch glimpses of it?

Where do I go to access it?

Read *John 7:37,38*

How do I know it is there?

Why are the outlets often scary looking?

What "outlets of living water" in my life have had scary faces?

Am I shunning them because of their face? Where have I learned to look past the scary face to receive the water?

What outlets have had kind, inviting faces? How has the water been different from these?

Would I stay in the cottage by myself given the chance? Why or why not?

What would I write on the wall of the cottage after staying for a few days?

How long would I wait before returning to read what I had written?

Dream Boxes

I *carefully folded my dreams and placed them between sheets of scented tissue paper in a clean white box on the shelf beside grandma's hand me down lace and still unused wedding gifts. It was not the first time I had put something in that box. It would not be the last. Each one had a story, a moment of insight or desire, a motive and a decision.*

Even though I knew they were safe and that I could get them out sometime later it was with regret that I closed the door and turned my back on them.

How many dreams would I have to put away until someone else was taken care of, another crisis weathered, or sufficient resources gathered?

I knew I was not alone. Everyone had a box in their cupboard. But that did not ease the grief and sense of loss I felt. Those were their dreams. These were mine.

One quiet Saturday morning I got the box down again and began to look through it. There were quite a lot of things in there and I was curious.

I carried the box to my room and locked the door. These were too personal for even those closest to me to see. I had never shown them to any one and felt strangely reticent to do so now.

Carefully unfolding each piece I examined them for signs of wear. Some were fraying at the corners. Others looked brand new. Not necessarily more recent, just more timely. I passed my fingers over them lightly for they seemed very fragile.

I took the timely ones and laid them end-to-end. What themes and patterns stood out? It was like looking at a scrapbook of my soul. Snapshots and images of what mattered to me, of what could have been, of what might be yet.

Some made me cry. It was bittersweet to think of them. Memories of people and places associated with those dreams washed over me. Cathartic and tender.

Some were delightful and fun. I remembered daring to dream them once. They were the mini skirts and fast cars of my dreams and I reveled in the luxury and rebelliousness of them. These dreams represented the adolescent side of my soul. Although I would deny these most vehemently if asked they secretly appealed to me in ways the others never could.

Buried at the bottom of the box were "the other kind" of dreams. They took a while to find for they were hidden best of all. They were wrapped in many layers and I handled them carefully. I was more afraid of and embarrassed by these few than all the rest together. I simultaneously loved and hated them. I knew they were the dreams that really counted but they would cost so much! They had the potential to heal so much and hurt so badly. I had watched others fall in the pursuit of like ideals. They haunted and intrigued me and I could neither look at them fully nor hide them away again.

What should I do now with all of these— laid bare before me? Could I afford to keep any out? Could I afford to put them all away? Suddenly I did not have the time or energy to decide. I quickly packed them up again, burying the deepest ones down out of reach, lightly running my hand over the fun and frivolous ones, kissing some before I placed them, one on top of another in the box.

I told myself, "Another day."

Placing the box safely back on the shelf next to grandma's lace I wondered what her dreams must have been. What had happened to her dream box? Sadly I realized I would never know now. I stood very still for several minutes— then reached up and pulled my box out again. I did not want my granddaughter's to regret what I could have dared for them. I opened the box...

Journal Questions:

If I were to open my dream box what fanciful dreams might I find there?

What dreams excite me the most?

Why have I hidden them?

What are my "fun dreams"— the one's that represent my adolescent side?

What are my "bittersweet" dreams— the ones that make me laugh and cry?

What dreams have I kept that are fraying around the edges— no longer important to me and taking up space for what might be more timely or meaningful?

What deep and dangerous— even noble— dreams have I hidden deep inside my dream box?

Why am I not pursuing them?

Who would I be willing to pursue them for?

Who would I be if I were pursuing them?

How will I know when it is time?

Is it possible one of them might be my calling?

If our true life work is truly a calling, who is it that calls? Who is the Architect behind our very best dreams? The dreams that invite us to make a difference?

And, if there is such an Architect, how am I accessing the "blue-prints"?

How open am I to be changed by the journey following these dreams would involve?

"Is it possible to become more intentional about creating spaces
—in relationship, in community—
where our fearful shadows can emerge into the light
to be seen for what they are, where the truth and love within us
can appear and make a claim on our lives?

We obviously are expert at creating spaces of other sorts.

We know, for example, how to create spaces that invite the intellect to
show up,
analyzing reality, parsing logic, and arguing its case.

We know how to invite the emotions into play,
reacting to injury, expressing anger, and celebrating joy.

We know how to invite the will to emerge, consolidating
energy and effort on behalf of a common task.

We know beyond doubt how
to invite the ego to put in an appearance, polishing its image, protect-
ing
its turf, and demanding its rights!

But we seem to know very little about
creating spaces that invite the soul to make itself known."

—Parker J. Palmer

My hope is that these journals have given you space to truly breathe... safe spaces where your soul could reflect and explore ... home places where your soul could rest and play... gentle, whimsical, places where you could create and dream.

In a world where such places are uncommon I commend your desire for a truly rich life.

Go in peace and remember to breathe deeply,

E.O.H. MacDonald

Printed in Great Britain
by Amazon